A Millennial's Guide to Breaking into Medical Device Sales

A Millennial's Guide to Breaking into Medical Device Sales

#WinYourSalesCareer

David Bagga

Copyright © 2017 David Bagga
All rights reserved.

ISBN: 1544705549
ISBN 13: 9781544705545

Dedication

To: ALL the medical device sales candidates across the country. I wrote this for everyone out there seeking their dream sales job and hoping to find success in their sales career. I hope this book will serve as a guide and help every medical device sales candidate out there and every person wanting to get into the medical device sales industry and *WIN YOUR* medical device sales career.

> "Sales is the world's highest paid profession, IF we're good at it, and IF we know where we're going."
> – Earl Nightengale

INTRODUCTION

Hey everyone! David Bagga here, I want to first say thank you to everybody that purchased my book **"A MILLENNIAL'S Guide To Breaking Into Medical Device Sales".** My ultimate goal is to help as many candidates as I can out there trying to break into this awesome sales industry of medical devices, and ultimately give you guys the tools to get the job you want and have an awesome career in medical device sales. I want to be a resource for everyone out there, point you all on the right path, and eventually watch all of you take off and fly into a successful career in the medical device sales industry.

I decided to write this book because every week as a medical device sales recruiter, I receive dozens of phone calls, Linked-In messages/In-Mails and hundreds of emails from candidates across the country asking questions, sending resumes, and most commonly – looking for advice from a medical sales recruiter on how to get their foot in the door to the medical device sales industry and what the path to the medical device sales industry looks like.

I realized the best way to help everyone out there with questions is to take the knowledge that I've learned as a hardcore medical device and B2B sales recruiter and share it with everyone with the hopes that it will help springboard you guys into the medical device sales industry once there's an understanding of what you actually need to do. Before we get into our agenda that consists of the medical sales industry itself, the interview process, the right resume, and winning your medical device sales career, I want to share my story and my motivation with all of you.

In early 2010, I had just gotten cut from playing professional basketball in England. My dream of being a professional athlete had come to a screeching halt and suddenly I found myself asking the dreaded question every recent college graduate faces – *"What am I going to do with my life?"*

Ordinarily, any 23 year old would be looking forward to transitioning to a life after college to see what the next chapter is, but given the state of the economy at the time (the economy crashed in 2008) and seeing how bleak the job market was, I was in limbo, and not too many people outside of my parents were offering advice or suggestions. The most common suggestion I heard was "Go back to school and get your MBA, it's the safest thing to do".

Most of my professors, academic advisors, coaches, college basketball teammates and people I met at the University of Arizona over my 4 year college experience told me I'd make a great outside sales rep because I had a big presence when I entered a room (I'm 6'5), smiled constantly, and had an unusual ability to approach and talk to anyone at any given point (I majored in communications). It was definitely something to think about, but a hardcore sales career had never crossed my mind because as a college athlete, you're living an unusually hectic life that consists of balancing an academic schedule with an athletic schedule, basically I had a full time job while I was a college student for 4 years.

One night out, post college graduation and pursuing professional basketball overseas, I ran into someone I knew with his wife. She saw the way I interacted with everyone I had just met and eventually asked me 15-20 minutes into the conversation, "have you ever thought about a career in medical device sales before?" "Not really", I replied. "Well, our company is hiring and I can get you a job so you can make a lot of money and make your parents proud", she said with extreme confidence.

I wasn't really into this whole medical device career conversation until I heard "our top reps make over $300K/year and have a great lifestyle", and then I started nodding, smiling, and offered to pay for everyone's dinner with absolutely no money. Not only was I intrigued, I was all-in and ready to get this job.

A few days went by and I looked over the website she emailed me, and made flash-cards to prepare myself on the basics (company info, what they sell, when they were founded, who the founder was, etc.) and asked her a few times before I interviewed "How do I get this job and what do I need to know?" "Don't worry", she said. "All you need to do is talk to the sales manager about how being a college athlete made you disciplined and gave you a great work ethic and you should be good to go to get a spot on our sales team". I was told my interview would last for 1 hour with a sales manager and the next step would be shadowing a rep from the company to get a feel for the job.

My first interview was in a conference room at a local hotel and as I walked in, I was greeted by the sales manager I was told about, and her boss, the VP of sales who I wasn't told would be there. As the interview started, questions about my knowledge of the medical device industry, the products capabilities, the call points of the product/job, and situational questions were being asked left and right. I didn't have an answer to anything and slowly my confidence was dwindling. My eyes were all over the place, constantly looking at my watch and the wall clock behind the 2 decision makers and at one point I started to question internally why this was happening to me.

It was evident that not only was I unprepared, I wasn't going to pass this interview let alone get this medical device sales job. The VP of sales stopped the interview 15-20 minutes in and said to me "young man, you have the potential to be an amazing sales rep and successful at whatever you do, but you have to be prepared for these interviews and understand what it takes to succeed in this industry and it's evident that you are not prepared to win your career". He immediately stood up, extended his hand, and thanked me for coming, then walked out of the room.

My confidence was shattered. I took off my jacket, undid my tie from my suit and couldn't face anyone after that interview. I was embarrassed and broken, but after a few days went by and I looked myself in the mirror, I found motivation after I thought about what this VP of sales told me about a winning a sales career.

I share this story with every candidate I have placed or continue to place across the country in the medical device industry because I made a promise when I became a medical device/b2b sales recruiter, to never let this type of scenario happen to any candidate interviewing for a medical device/life science sales job I submit them for. That is my motivation for doing this. I want to make sure every candidate reading this is not only prepared to interview, but prepared to WIN your interview, WIN your sales job, and ultimately WIN your medical device/next level sales career.

Table of Contents

Dedication · v

Introduction ·ix

Chapter 1   Why pursue a sales career? The facts about what hardcore sales can do for you · · · · · · · 1

Chapter 2   Why Medical Device Sales? What can the Industry do for You as a Candidate? · · · · · · · 7

Chapter 3   The Medical Device Sales Resume and How to Structure Your Resume the Right Way · · · 15

Part 1   Contact information and Objective statement · 18

Part 2   Experience · 23

XV

Part 3	Education and Extracurricular activities	28
Chapter 4	The Phone Interview	31
Chapter 5	The Face-To-Face Interview	39
Chapter 6	The Field Ride/Day In the Life of a Medical Device Sales Rep	57
Chapter 7	The Final Interview	64
Chapter 8	The Right Profile and Path to take to Breaking into Medical Device Sales	70
Chapter 9	The Millennial Effect in Sales	82
Chapter 10	My Closing Words	85

CHAPTER 1

WHY PURSUE A SALES CAREER? THE FACTS ABOUT WHAT HARDCORE SALES CAN DO FOR YOU

> "If you make yourself more than just a man, if you devote yourself to an ideal, and if they can't stop you, then you become something else entirely."
> – LIAM NIESSAN AS RAS'AL-GHUL IN "*BATMAN BEGINS*"

Have you ever seen the hit movie *Batman Begins*? It stars Christian Bale as Batman and Liam Niesen as the super-villain Ras-Al-Ghul. 15 minutes into the movie, there's an excellent scene when a tired, physically worn-out Bruce Wayne accepts a challenge from Ras-Al-Ghul in a local jail cell in India about finding the right path in his life. Ras-Al-Ghul challenges Bruce Wayne to find a rare blue flower on top of a mountain and hand-deliver it to him if he's serious about finding the right path for his life.

Wayne climbs the mountain, grabs the blue Poppy flower, and delivers it to Ras-Al-Ghul in his training facility, fulfilling the wish of Ras-Al-Ghul and leading him to start his training of becoming Batman. However, before he begins his training; Ras-Al-Ghul, joined by his team of warriors from the League of Shadows looks into the eyes of Bruce Wayne and asks him *"WHAT ARE YOU SEEKING?"*

Wayne tells Ras-Al-Ghul his answer about what he's ultimately seeking, hands him the blue poppy flower he was challenged to find, and Ras-Al-Ghul follows up with the question *"ARE YOU READY TO BEGIN?"* Before Wayne can get out his next answer, Ras-Al-Ghul kicks him as hard as he can in the chest and says *"Death does not wait for you to be ready! Death is not considerate at all!"* And then follows that up with another hard kick to Wayne's chest and says *"And make no mistake in here you'll face the true challenges of Death!"*, meaning that he has to be prepared for everything and know what path he's seeking in his life.

The world of hardcore sales is similar in many ways to this brief and powerful scene from *Batman Begins*. The sales world does not wait for us to be ready, and it's not considerate to any of us at all, unless we consistently perform at a high level. As potential candidates, before you break into the medical device sales industry or any hardcore sales industry, you have to know what you're seeking, what your purpose is, and more importantly, how you're going to find success as a hardcore sales rep.

Earl Nightengale has a great quote from his audio program "The Strangest Secret in the World", saying **"Selling is the world's highest paid profession, IF we're good at it, and if we know where we're going**. Think about his quote for a second; so many people across the world want to get into the hardcore sales arena and find success, but they have no direction, no purpose, and they wind up drifting aimlessly from job to job and their career winds up passing them by. But as candidates, if you know the right path to an unusually unique industry such as medical device sales, know how to get there, and know what's expected from you, the challenge becomes less challenging, more exciting and ultimately rewarding in the end for you.

The world of hardcore sales can be rewarding on many levels. It allows you to meet with people daily, provide products/services to organizations, advance in the workforce, and provides a lifestyle and compensation that most people are seeking.

But, to be a great hardcore sales rep or what is known as a "Rainmaker", you have to be prepared to do things like train extensively, condition your mind to sell, learn about the products/services you're selling, prospect for new business daily (hello cold-calling), honor the sales process, sell/produce annually, and most importantly; find the industry that suits your personality and gets you fired up to sell daily. Here are 5 key reasons why a sales career is great and why you should want to break into the awesome world of sales.

1. **Money** – in the world of sales, you're almost guaranteed to make more money selling than you are in an administrative or office job, but only if you deliver results. Any company (medical device, b2b, or start-up) needs to make money to survive and if the reps are great at producing sales, they're usually rewarded. And it's usually safe to say the better the sales rep, the more money the rep will earn. According to simplyhired.com, the average sales salary came in at $60K/year with a high of $160K/year. Of course everything depends on years of experience, job title, industry, and obviously if you are delivering results.

2. **Road to Management** – Most c-level executives or "higher ups" usually have spent some time in sales at some point during their career. Why? Well it's simple, no matter what your job in business winds up being; you're always selling something whether it's to your boss, a colleague, your company or customers. The qualities/traits you've learned from being any type of hardcore sales rep will carry over to a management level job.

3. **YOU are in control** – Sales gives you the flexibility to run your own day, especially outside sales. You control your schedule, when you meet with clients, when you sell and more importantly, you can control your own destiny as long as you're delivering results on an annual basis.

4. **Security of your own job** – No matter what the state of the economy is, sales reps will always have job security. Even If you lose your sales job or decide to leave early, you'll have no problem finding another sales job based off a proven track record of success and what you've learned from prior sales experiences to springboard you forward throughout your sales career. Successful sales reps should always be able to find another sales job and make a living comfortably in the world of sales.
5. **It's fun**! – Sales is supposed to be fun! It's fun to meet clients, show them who you are, represent the company you sell for, build relationships, get educated on products/services, and eventually have fun while selling to the world, and of course, it's always fun to get paid handsomely for your ability to sell something to a business and be great at what you do. Once you understand the marketplace and what purpose your product/service serves and then sell those product/services to clients and businesses, sales winds up becoming fun and very rewarding.

Action Items – Why Pursue a Sales Career?

1. Ask yourself "What type of career are you seeking for yourself?"
2. Do you have a personality to sell and deal with the responsibilities of selling and delivering results everyday?

3. Have you ever considered hardcore sales? If not, why not? What is holding you back from taking that leap of faith and breaking into the world of sales?
4. Can you see yourself enjoying the challenge of selling and everything that comes with that career?

CHAPTER 2

WHY MEDICAL DEVICE SALES? WHAT CAN THE INDUSTRY DO FOR YOU AS A CANDIDATE?

> "A goal without a plan is just a wish"
> – ANTOINE DE SAINT-EXUPERY

There's an old saying about popularity. Everyone wants to be a part of something popular, be associated with someone popular, or part of the "In Crowd" because it's popular, but they don't know how to join a popular club. In the chapter 1 we discussed the important question "Why Sales?" and I listed some critical reasons for people to break into a sales career and what a career in outside sales can do you for you from a lifestyle standpoint and a career standpoint. In this chapter, I want to go over why the medical device sales industry is so popular and the reasons why people want to join the medical device sales industry

The medical device industry in a nutshell is like being part of an elite fraternity: Once you become a member/

sales rep, you'll be selling for a great company, industry, and more importantly you'll be extremely successful and it will open a good amount of doors up for you throughout your medical device sales career, and more importantly, you'll be a part of something popular and that can help a sales rep with many things like confidence, happiness, will to be successful, etc.

There are so many different directions you can go in the medical device industry. For example, there's OR (Operating Room) sales, surgical sales, capital equipment sales, disposable sales, oncology, neurology, aesthetic equipment, etc. and that's only a few divisions, there's hundreds more.

Did you know the medical device industry generates over $90B/year and there are over 90K jobs every year? That's not a typo, over 90K jobs/year! Think about that for a few seconds, pretty crazy right? It's our job as medical device sales recruiters to help fill those job openings with the right people for the right organizations. Here are some reasons why people love working in the medical device sales industry:

1. **<u>Unlimited growth potential</u>** – As hardcore sales reps, when you're entering that big next step of your sales career you don't want to be capped on anything (especially income and growth) and you want to know the potential to grow is there, and the medical device sales industry provides unlimited growth to every rep that enters in. I tell candidates all the time

via phone when I'm screening them for medical jobs I'm filling that these medical device companies "don't set you up to fail, they set you up to grow and succeed, BUT it's up to you to take their plan they've given you as a medical device sales rep and run with it in stride." I say this because even though people know there's unlimited growth potential in medical device sales, to grow with a company, it still falls on you the sales rep to perform and exceed the expectations an organization has for you.

2. **Flexible Schedule/Hours** – A lot of reps I've placed in my time as being a medical sales recruiter value the medical device industry because of the flexibility it gives them, and the flexibility that comes with their jobs. It's important to remember in hardcore medical device sales jobs, there might not be a local office you're checking into everyday, meaning you as the sales rep, will have more flexibility to make your own hours and handle your business. BUT, it's important to note that the top-performing medical device sales reps are usually always in the field working, building relationships, prospecting, selling, and most importantly closing and delivering results. Sometimes I've heard medical device reps say that there's a feeling of being self-employed because they don't see their boss everyday or they're hopping on a plane to cover part of their multi-state territory which can be a benefit to the job.

3. **Clients/Relationships** – A lot of medical device reps enjoy the clients that turn into customers in the industry and the relationships they build with these customers. There's a healthy amount of the doctors, nurses, HR staff, and c-level decision makers that will wind up meeting you, buying from you, recommending you/your product service, and then use your product/service on patients in a hospital or the desired call point that you're calling on as a sales rep. The big difference between a lot of medical device sales jobs and B2B sales jobs like payroll, uniform, and copier sales jobs is that medical device sales jobs are what I call an R.D.S also known as a Relationship-Driven Sale. A b2b job is more transactional and after you sell the product/service, you're onto the next account or next client and there's no real relationship that gets built. A medical device job is about building long-term relationships with this hospital, doctor, or call point. A lot of feedback I get from medical sales reps is that they genuinely enjoy the medical device sales industry because of the relationships they wind up building and then turning those relationships into sales and later on referrals.

4. **Territory Management** – One of the first answers I usually get from sales reps when I ask them why they want to break into medical sales is "I want a bigger/sexier territory than the 5-10 zip codes I have at my

outside B2B sales job now." In my opinion running a big territory, or managing and growing a multi-state territory like California, Nevada, Arizona, Colorado and Utah is a huge selling point and it's a big perk to the job. In a way when you have a territory that big you get an opportunity to become the "Mayor of your territory" and you become the boss. You as the sales rep become the relationship builder, the closer, the difference maker, and more importantly you become the one responsible for growing the territory. You're not drying up or saturating your territory over and over again. Depending on the medical device company and the sales position you wind up winning, there's usually a lot less bodies in bigger territories too which allows you as the sales rep to become the go-to person that people rely on in that territory.

5. **MONEY** – Obviously money and the income potential you can make as a hardcore medical device sales rep is important when you're trying to break into this industry. A lot of reps I've placed in the medical device sales industry notice that in medical device the cliché is true: "The harder I work, the more money I earn." With sales reps, money is a tool for building self-esteem weekly/monthly/yearly, and if you work hard in this industry, you will earn a good amount of money and become a successful medical device sales rep. I remember when

I was working as an outside sales rep at a fortune 500 B2B payroll company, my regional zone manger told me if I worked harder than the other reps on the teams I'd make right around $105K which was over 100% of the YTD plan. There were over 60 of us in our branch/zone and at the time there were only 5-6 reps that were making $100K or more. The rest of us had to scrape and claw to make $70-80K and come close to hitting our year end goals. What you'll typically find in a B2B company's sales force is that usually 10% or less of the sales reps are making great money. Think about this, a 2015 survey said the average b2b/outside sales rep or median makes right around $68K with the top 10% of outside sales reps making roughly around $115K. However, In medical device sales, what we found was that the way the companies structure the comp plan/perks, usually about 30% of the sales force is making a great income. In 2016, a report from a medreps.com (A medical device job board which I highly recommend using by the way) noted that the average income for a medical device sales rep was right around $137K with a base right around $73K.

6. **Making a Difference** – Okay, so this might not be the "top reason" to get into medical device sales, some people might list a better paycheck or company car plus a gas card, but it certainly is a big reason why a lot of people want to break into medical device sales

and why the industry is so popular. I feel it everyday and I'm on the recruiting side of the medical device industry, so imagine how the reps feel that are catering to these call points like hospitals, operating rooms, nursing homes, wellness centers, etc. Think about this for a second, if you break into the medical device industry, you might get the opportunity to sell devices/medical services that change or even save people's lives daily. This is the one industry where that has the potential to happen everyday of your work week. I've heard medical device sales reps tell me that they'll make a sale on a piece of equipment with a doctor, and that piece of equipment will be used in surgery and it will help someone that's in pain or needs it and knowing they were a part of that process is a big deal because you're saving someone's life and you're making a huge difference. I think it's important to note that there's a sense of pride that comes with selling these medical devices/services too and it's something you can be proud of knowing you're making a difference as a medical device sales rep for years to come.

7. **U.S. Market is the Best Market for Medical Device Sales Reps** – The U.S. is the market and innovative leader in many things, including the medical device/life sciences space and has been for quite some time now. As potential medical device sales reps, there's no better market to sell into than the U.S.

market because you're working in an industry and a country with exponential growth rate year over year. It's important to think about the future growth rate and being a part of that growth rate, especially for millennials since more than 50% of the U.S. workforce will be millennials by the year 2020.

Action Items – Why Medical Device Sales?

1. What are your thoughts on the medical device sales industry after learning more about the industry and why people make a career/living out of it?
2. Do you see yourself finding success in the medical device sales industry?
3. What makes you want to start a career in medical device sales?
4. What questions do you have about the medical device sales industry?

CHAPTER 3

THE MEDICAL DEVICE SALES RESUME AND HOW TO STRUCTURE YOUR RESUME THE RIGHT WAY

> *"This is not just a resume, but the evolution of passion throughout the years of diligent work on the way to becoming an expert."*
> – NGENIOUS ART

Have any of you ever been waiting in line at a popular night club, bar, or an event that takes a while to get into? Sometimes it takes hours; maybe even all night and eventually you start to ask yourself "How long is it going to take me to get in here?" Then as you say that, you see a random person come up to the front of the line and pull out a VIP card and the door opens up and that person gets access to the place that you're trying to get into. You start to think to yourself "what does that person have that I don't have? Why are they letting this person into the sought after place and not me?"

In a unique way, the medical device sales industry is like that popular night club, bar, or event people try to get into every day. It's fun, exciting, and filled with opportunities that can help you the candidate get to the next step of your sales career and find the success you're looking for. The people waiting in line are like the thousands of candidates that apply weekly to a medical device sales position on a company's website and sometimes wait for weeks, months, maybe even a year to hear some type of feedback from someone with hopes of breaking into the medical device sales industry.

The VIP pass for getting your foot into the medical device sales industry is the sales resume. In a nutshell, the purpose of a sales resume is to provide an employer with a summary of your skills, abilities, and more importantly your accomplishments that make you the candidate stand out on paper. It really gives the employer and person you are interviewing with a "snapshot" of who you are, where you've been, what you've accomplished, where you were educated, and more importantly, **WHAT YOU BRING TO THE ORGANIZATION and WHY THEY SHOULD HIRE YOU**.

If someone looks great on paper, managers and employers will welcome a candidate with open arms to interview for a sales position on their team, with hopes that they are even better in person and wind up being everything the employer is looking for.

Keep in mind, there is no "perfect resume" out there and there's no perfect way to construct a resume. As candidates, especially to all the candidates that have 2-3 years of sales experience, you want to do your best to keep it to no more than 1 page, if you have more experience than that, do your best to tailor it professionally even if it winds up being 2 pages long. The big thing employers look for is a clean resume that reads well from top to bottom and puts you in a position to be successful as a candidate during the interview. I've broken down the medical device sales resume into 3 simple parts that will make it easy for any candidate to follow and more importantly, it will give you the sales candidate, a better understanding of what medical device sales employers, managers, and recruiters are looking for from potential candidates in the medical device sales industry.

PART 1

CONTACT INFORMATION AND OBJECTIVE STATEMENT

When an employer looks at your resume, they're going to read it from top to bottom, so it's important that the resume is clean and accurate from top to bottom. The contact information is especially important. You want to make sure you have your name bolded and at the top for everyone to see – why?

Because right off the bat, it makes you stand out in a good way as a candidate and separates yourself from other people you're interviewing against (Always think about how to outwork your competition). Remember the smallest factors can be difference makers between you winning and losing the job. Managers remember things like that when they see someone's name at the top that's bolded and it's right there at the top to start off the resume. I always encourage candidates to be bold in their approach (especially when interviewing in the medical device industry) and having your name stand out helps with that. It's important to make sure your contact info is accurate too.

For example - If you're interviewing for a medical sales job in Orange County, CA and they see an address from another city or state there are going to be questions about where you really live, where you're trying to be, what you're trying to accomplish, etc. and it can cause a manager to potentially end an interview before you get into the important part of the interview. It's important for any candidate interviewing to have the contact info of where you are presently residing. Also, when it comes to your email and your phone number, make sure you have your personal number and personal email on there, **NOT YOUR WORK CONTACT INFO**. Employers are very thorough and they filter out emails from sales recruiters and it's a risk that's not worth taking, so It's important you always use your personal contact info on your resume.

The Objective Statement – This is one of my favorite parts of the resume. It introduces you to the manager or the person you're interviewing with and shares a little bit about yourself before getting to your experience. In a nutshell, the objective statement on a resume is a two sentence breakdown that's meant for you to share what you're seeking in your sales career and how your previous experience throughout your career and throughout your life will help you find success at the future employer you're interviewing with.

As a medical sales recruiter, I always stress to candidates to have no more than a two sentence profile statement, especially if your resume is going to be no more than a page because you can only fit so much on there and you want the objective statement to be quick and to the point. The first sentence should say what you the sales candidate are seeking and what your expectations are from the employer. The second sentence should be about your prior experience and how that will help you find success wherever you wind up getting a respected job at.

For example, if you are an outside B2B rep looking to break into medical sales, you want to talk about how you are seeking an outside sales rep position where growth and compensation are based on performance. In the second sentence, take your prior sales experience and accomplishments and use that to do a "soft close" on the decision maker, the profile statement should leave the employer wanting to know more about you as you go forward in the interview, it helps for building a rapport with managers, finding a common ground, and gives you something to talk about with the manager/decision maker from the content in the statement.

It's important to note that I stay away from specifying industries to break into on the objective statement, because I've seen a few scenarios in the past where candidates will interview for a medical device sales job and they might accidently bring a resume that has "pharmaceutical sales" in their objective statement or vice versa, small errors like this can make you look un-prepared and may cause a manager to abruptly end an interview, but as a candidate, you should do what makes you feel comfortable.

My recommendation for sales candidates would be to keep it basic and simply put **"I am seeking an outside sales representative position..."** and go from there. If t helps, I used my profile statement below from when I was a medical device sales candidate so everyone can use it as a guide to help them out, and you can add your own style to it. The takeaways from my profile statement are that it shows what I'm seeking in my sales career, what my expectations are from the employer, and I used my previous experience as an outside sales rep and a former college/pro athlete to close the manager and show them what I bring to the organization and why they should hire me for the job.

YOUR NAME HERE

Address

City, State Zip

Phone – Direct/Cell

e-mail

OBJECTIVE

I am Seeking an outside sales representative position within a growth oriented company where advancement and earnings are based upon performance and achievement. My experience as a top performing outside sales rep at a fortune 500 company and prior experience as a former Pro/College athlete will help me succeed at any level.

PART 2

EXPERIENCE

This is the "core" of the medical device sales resume. The experience section on a resume separates the great candidates from the good candidates during an interview process, and remember, your goal is to not be good but to be great so you'll win the job. It's important for candidates to put their relevant experience under their objective statement since that's what employers are going to want to see and go over with you during the interview. It is ideal you put every company you've worked at since graduating college. If you are in college or recently graduated (6 months -1 year) then apply the same technique and talk about your internships and how you performed during those opportunities.

A lot of times, candidates will put different titles next to the jobs they had. For example, sometimes payroll reps will put "district sales manager" or "major market sales manager" which is fine, but essentially they're all the same thing. I typically suggest any type of outside sales rep simplify it and put the phrase "Territory Sales Representative" or "Outside

Territory Representative" next to the company you work at then elaborate about it to a manager that's interviewing you. The reason why is because you can explain to the manager what division you are a part of, what responsibilities you have, and most importantly, what your achievements have been during your tenure with the organization. I also recommend for each company you've worked at to put the call point of the product/service you're selling. Managers are smart but we can't assume they know everything about us and our occupation by just looking at our resume.

For example, if you're selling something like payroll, a product that has multiple divisions in companies, then you should indicate everything in a bullet point by saying something quick and to the point like **"Responsible for selling major market payroll, HCM, and HR solutions to medium-large size businesses across my assigned territory of Orange County, CA."** Right off the bat, this tells the manager what you're calling on, what you're selling, what your territory is and what your overall responsibilities are in one bullet point. As candidates, you can't assume managers know what you're selling and what you're calling on so it's important that you have that documented in the experience section of the resume because it gives the manager a clear picture of what you're doing and what your responsibilities are.

The most important part of the experience section (and resume in general) on a sales resume are the accomplishments and awards you've received throughout your career with employers, sales experience is great but it doesn't mean anything without the accomplishments you've achieved. Why is this so important? Well, think about it from this perspective.

Managers will never tell you this as candidates but one of their main jobs is to make sure the sales goals are not just met, but exceeded on a monthly/quarterly/yearly basis, so if you as a candidate can list all the goals and accomplishments you've exceeded, then you'll separate yourself from the competition going into a medical device sales interview, and you'll give yourself a better chance at winning the job (Always remember to think about how you can out-work your competition).

Like I said earlier in this chapter, the medical device sales industry is an elite, exclusive and selective sales club to be a part of and one of the things they're extremely picky about is sales numbers and achievements on a resume. Responsibilities are great but achievements and sales rankings always outweigh the responsibilities. Medical device companies want people that have not only hit their sales quotas but exceeded everything in their path and have shattered their competition.

Some companies document everything and recognize top performing sales reps. Even if your current employer doesn't recognize everything or document employee's success, you should be able to put down the years that you were able to achieve/exceed quotas annually, monthly, quarterly, etc. It's important to document things like sales contests, recognition from management and any other award that your company keeps track of to put it down on your resume, why? Because it separates yourself from the competition. If you have a resume with no achievements and no responsibilities, chances are managers won't want to take a chance on you because there's no proven track record of success in your career.

I tell candidates to think of the experience part of a sales resume like New England Patriots QB Tom Brady's football trading card. It's filled with numerous achievements, awards, all types of numbers, and stats. Any medical device employer will want to see the same thing from great candidates that are interviewing for their respected sales positions.

I put a section from our sample sales resume here below for everyone to check out and use as a guide, so going forward, you know how to structure the experience section on your sales resume. If you notice the first thing that stands out are the bullet points on both sales positions are mostly achievements, awards, and stats. Responsibilities are great but as I said earlier in this chapter, achievements always outweigh responsibilities.

EXPERIENCE

Paychex   **Orange County, CA**
Major Account Executive   **Feb 2012-Present**
Territory Rep

- #1/385 Sales Representative in nation 2013 – 10 out of 12 months

- #1/15 Sales Representative Producer in Irvine Office 2005 YTD
- Ranked in the top 15/385 Sales Representatives Nationwide 2005 YTD
- Highest Net Revenue Award October 2013 – 675% over quota
- Circle of Excellence Award (presidents club) – 2013
- Surpassed expected quota FY' 2012- 200%
- Promoted to Major Account Executive after 9 Months (competed against and beat out every rep in the territory to win this promotion)

ADP **Los Angeles, CA**
Territory Rep **March 2010 - January 2012**

- Top Closer 2010-2011 out of 12 in rookie class/increased revenue 30%
- Sales Representative of the Month Award in March, April and May 2011
- Rookie of the quarter in Q1 of 2011 with over 117% of YTD goal and over $40K in revenue brought in

PART 3

EDUCATION AND EXTRACURRICULAR ACTIVITIES

Finally, we can't forget about our education or extracurricular activities on our sales resume. I always recommend candidates put their education and activities at the bottom of their sales resumes instead of the top. Reason being is because most employers require a 4 year bachelors degree but they value your sales experience and your accomplishments more as you climb the sales ladder throughout your career.

When it comes to your extracurricular activities from your time in school or something that you're doing now; think about what you were or are involved in outside of your job and how you can use the activity to springboard yourself into a medical device sales job. For example, when I was interviewing as a sales candidate, I was able to use my experience playing professional and college basketball and talk about the qualities I learned daily as student-athlete, how I applied it to my sales career, and how it made me a better sales rep.

I used this to help sell myself to employers I was interviewing with. Every candidate can use an extracurricular activity and use that as a selling point when you're interviewing for a medical device sales job so it's important you put them on your resume and be proud of what you've accomplished. Remember, how you sell yourself along with positioning your extracurricular activities will make a manager take notice during the interview process.

Part 3 of the sample medical device sales resume below shows the education and extracurricular section from the sample sales resume. It's important to note things that will stand out to an employer like the GPA that you maintained while you were in school and any awards you received in school should go down as well. Also, any clubs you were a part of should go under the achievements section below your education. It's important to stress the day-to-day activities of the extracurricular activities you were a part of, what you learned, and how you can apply those to your sales job. All of these achievements will give you a better chance to springboard yourself into the medical device sales industry.

EDUCATION

University of Arizona   **May 2009**

- Bachelor of Arts, Communications
- Graduated in top 5% of graduating class in 2009
- Graduated Summa Cum Laude 3.5 GPA

ATHLETIC ACHIEVEMENTS

- Member of British Basketball League New Castle Eagles during 2009-10 season, averaged 24PPG and led team in 3 point percentage
- Member of the University of Arizona men's basketball team 2005-09
- Captain of Basketball Team, 2008-2009
- All-Academic Pac-10 – 2008 and 2009 (3.5GPA)
- University of Arizona Senior Scholar Athlete of the Year, 2009

Action Items – Medical Device Sales resume

1. How does your sales resume compare with your peers?
2. Compare your sales resume to someone you know that is successful and can offer constructive criticism
3. Do your sales achievements outweigh your sales responsibilities on your resume? If not, what can you add to improve your resume?
4. Is your resume` ready for submission after you make the necessary changes?

CHAPTER 4

THE PHONE INTERVIEW

> "Success always comes when
> preparation meets opportunity."
> – Henry Hartman

Remember what it's like to have that initial first date with someone you're really trying to start a relationship with? There's a certain plan you're trying to follow. You want to look your best, be early, show that you're interested in what they're saying, let your great side come out, etc. More importantly, your big goal is to get another date with that person so you can show the person what you potentially bring to the relationship and ultimately if all goes according to plan, start a relationship with that person you admire.

Interviewing is a lot like dating. It's an opportunity that's exciting, overwhelming, has a process, and someone will make a decision about you after a few interviews to determine if you're the person for their organization. There can be a good number of steps throughout the medical device interview process which include:

- The Phone Interview/Phone Screen
- On-line profile/personality test
- Face-to-Face Interviews with managers
- Ride-Along/Field rides with sales reps
- Final Interview with the VP of Sales or Regional Sales Director

Preparing your best will be required throughout the interview process, and remember, the better you prepare, the more of a chance you give yourself to WIN your sales job and ultimately WIN your sales career. Everyday when I'm prepping candidates over the phone I constantly remind them to prepare 110% and separate themselves from the competition during the interview process because managers/decision makers have a difficult time deciding on who they're going to hire for the sales jobs since there are so many interviews going on, but if you're more prepared than your competition, then you'll make a managers decision a lot easier.

It's important to remember that sales managers hire candidates they like and think are best fit to handle the job that's on the table, so from a candidate's perspective it's important to connect with the manager during the interview process on some level.

I've broken down every step of the interview process for medical device sales jobs below here for you to review and apply the tips as you start the interview process. In this chapter we'll go over how to prepare for the phone interview, tips for winning the phone interview, and tips for closing for the next steps of the interview process which is the face-to-face interview.

The Phone Interview – Sometimes, managers will start the interview process with a 30-40 minute phone interview before they bring the candidate in for a face-to-face interview. It can be challenging without the right preparation. The biggest challenge candidate's face is trying to understand the person interviewing you over the phone since you can't see them face-to-face and see the expressions on their face.

Tips for *WINNING* the Phone Interview

1. **BE ON TIME**! – If the hiring manager or a representative from the employer is calling you, make sure you give yourself at least a 20-30 minute window incase the manager calls you early. When decision makers call and candidates are late or don't answer on time, employers minds are already made up which is why it's important to always be on time, even for a phone interview. Remember, being on time shows that you honor the interview process and winning your sales job is important to you.

2. **Do Your Research On the Company** – This is extremely important. Even though the traditional phone interview is about you and what you bring to the organization as a potential sales rep, you still want to be prepared 110% and do your research on the company that's interviewing you. Make sure to review the website thoroughly multiple times so you know it well and can answer questions with confidence. Looking up articles about the company and seeing current facts about them helps too. Preparing some questions to have is crucial so the person on the other end of the phone interviewing you knows you're serious about winning the phone interview and knows you've done your homework on the company.

3. **Take the attitude as if it were an in person interview** – If you don't pass the phone interview then you're done, there's no other way to say it. You can't win the job from a phone interview but you can certainly lose it, and the opportunity to get the dream sales job you've been looking for. Candidates throughout the country don't prepare enough for the phone interview because they treat it as "just a phone interview" and it hinders them from moving forward in the interview process. When a manager passes on someone after the phone screen it's usually because they're not prepared or weren't worth the manager to bring in for an in-person interview. Remember

you must be prepared even for the phone interview. Your ultimate goal during the phone interview is to close the manager over the phone for an in-person interview.

4. **Move around while you're on the phone talking to the MGR** – This helps your voice get stronger over the phone and it also helps give you confidence over the phone. I do it a lot while I'm screening candidates everyday and prepping them for interviews and I believe it helps the candidate as well while they're on the phone, it also gets your blood flowing and you can think quicker while you're moving around and talking and the interview will be flowing more while you're moving around.

5. **Wear Professional Attire** – We used to have an old saying when the newest basketball shoes came out I was playing division 1 college basketball, "If I look good I'm going to play good". The same principle applies to the interview process for hardcore medical device sales jobs, if you look the part, you'll give yourself a better chance of winning the part, even if it is over the phone. If you're ready to go and dressed in a suit or professional attire, you're mentality will be more professional over the phone as oppose to someone wearing a t-shirt and sweatpants that might come across as laid-back or casual, and there's nothing casual about being a sales rep in the world of hardcore medical device sales.

6. **Have your resume/brag book with you** – It's important that you're prepared to go over your resume from start to finish, even during a phone screen, and if you can talk about your awards to the person screening you that will help too; and it's important to remember not to forget your resume for a phone screen.

7. **Make sure you're in a quiet place** – You want to make sure you're not going to be distracted for a phone interview. If you can be in a place where it's quiet and you can lock the door so no one will bother you then you'll think more clear during the phone interview as oppose to having distractions or outside noise.

8. **No long-winded answers** – Most phone interviews last between 30 and 40 minutes. That's not enough time to give your life story to the hiring manager. It's Important to give short, crisp, and concise answers over the phone because the manager or representative from the employer screening you might have a set list of questions they want to go over with you.

9. **ALWAYS BE CLOSING**! – Remember to close the manager as hard as you can to get to next step of the interview process (usually a face-to-face interview). After the initial conversation ends, close the manager by asking him/her over the phone "After interviewing me today over the phone, what would your concerns be about moving me forward to the next

step of the interview process?" If there is pushback from the managers end, ask the manager about it, then close the manager again and ask when you can come in for a face-to-face interview, make the person on the phone see that you're serious about WINNING your sales job and WINNING your sales career.

10. **Thank you** – Before getting off the call with the interviewer it's important to ask for their email address and send them a follow-up "thank-you-email". In the thank you email, be sure to thank them for their time and remember to close them again on why they should bring you in for a face to face interview.

It's important to remember as candidates you have one goal – to WIN the phone interview and go into a face-to-face interview.

Action Items – The Phone Interview

1. Are you mentally preparing yourself for the phone interview and to start the interview process with an employer in the medical device arena? It's important to make sure you take the attitude as you would during a face to face interview.
2. Treat the person over the phone as the primary decision maker regardless of what their title is. It doesn't matter if the person screening you is from HR

(Human Resources) or a Regional Sales Director, it's crucial to your success to make sure you treat the person over the phone with respect, show professionalism, come prepared to go over your resume/work history and most importantly you **CLOSE** that person for the next steps of the interview process.

3. Have you been practicing mock phone interviews with successful reps in medical device sales and inquiring about how their phone interviews went with previous employers? This is vital to your success because if you can find reps that have been through the interview process and found success, they can share knowledge with you and it will help prepare you for the process.

CHAPTER 5

THE FACE-TO-FACE INTERVIEW

> "Let's face it: A date is a job interview
> that lasts all night. The only difference
> between a date and a job interview is:
> not many job interviews is there a chance
> you'll end up naked at the end of it"
> – JERRY SEINFELD

The **Face-To-Face Interview** – Now that you've passed the phone interview, you're moving on to the face-to-face part of the interview process. It's an exciting time for you as a professional medical device sales candidate, you're competing with other candidates and it's up to you to keep advancing in the interview process and "wow" the manager so you can WIN the job you want and springboard yourself to the sales career you want.

Meeting with a manager face-to-face is great because you get to bring your presence and your personality to the interview process and show the manager who you are in person and why they should hire you for the job. Most managers know in the first 3-5 minutes whether or not they're going to hire a candidate for a position, so it's important to have great body language, be energetic, look the part, and most importantly, come prepared to WIN. In this chapter I'll break down the tips for your face-to-face interview with sales managers, the right questions to ask them, and tips for advancing to the next round of the interview process which is the Ride-Along.

Here are some tips for WINNING the Face-To-Face Interview:

1. **<u>PREP YOURSELF!</u>** – Do your research in the days leading up to the face-to-face interview. A lot of times reading over the job description simply won't cut it with a big-time medical device company and their manager will know if you're just regurgitating the job description back to them. Read the company's website thoroughly; reach out to reps via linkedin or social media for advice before you go in for your interview, look up the products, new trends in the marketplace, how the company/products have evolved, and find success stories about the company you can share with the manager. Any hiring manager will appreciate the effort you put in as a candidate to win the job. If you're working with a recruiter that's placed candidates at the company before, ask the recruiter what previous candidates have done to win

the interview and how they separated themselves from the competition.

2. **<u>Be Prepared the Night Before/Morning Of</u>** – Get a good night's sleep (At least 8 hours of sleep) the night before your interview so you can be refreshed, laser focused, and full of energy when you meet with the hiring manager. It's important you eat a good breakfast the morning of the interview too. Having the right food in your body like healthy protein will help you have more stamina for a long interview, if you're a coffee drinker do not drink too much, have the right amount so you're not sounding hyper to a manager.

3. **<u>Do not Bail on the Interview or be a "No-Show"</u>** – This is one of the cardinal sins in the interview process and if it happens, it happens during the first face-to-face interview. Believe it or not, there are some sales candidates out there that will decide the job interview we put them into or connect them with isn't for them and medical device sales isn't for them, and that's okay. But, if you're a sales candidate and you decide to not show up to the interview the morning of or the night before, it will almost certainly eliminate you from the interview process before it even begins.

- Quick Story - In early 2015 we were recruiting for a fortune 500 medical device company that had a very well known reputation and the manager wanted to interview the group of candidates we had submitted to him later in the work week. The manager and our recruiting team made it clear to the candidates that the manager was flying in from another part of the country so they all had to be ready to interview, and if they couldn't make the interviews to let us know right away so we could notify the hiring manager. One of the candidates we were dealing with was an on-call rep from a another well-known medical device company and we said to the candidate from the beginning "If you can't make the interview that's 3 days from now, please let us know immediately and we will remove you from the interview process". The Candidate responded to our email quickly, "I'll be there and be ready to go". We prepped the candidate and supplied all the information of where to meet the manager and 15 minutes before the candidates interview was supposed to take place, we received a text message saying he couldn't make the interview. When we told the manager what had happened the manager asked for the candidates name so he could write it down. The manager then told me he would never interview that candidate again, no matter how desperate he got for great reps on his team. Unfortunately for the candidate, word of mouth traveled fast about the lack of communication skills that was displayed, and clients were hesitant to give the candidate an interview. The point of the story is that the hardcore medical sales industry is a small world, managers and decision maker's talk, and word travels fast about how you communicate, especially during the interview process. If you can't make it to an interview, always take the professional approach and contact the recruiter you're working with and the hiring manager if you can, and give them enough of a notice (not the day of or night before) saying you cannot make the interview. Remember, during the interview process, the smallest factors make the biggest difference between you winning and losing your job.

4. **Make your social media pages PRIVATE!** – This is a bigger deal than people think. The last thing you want is to start an interview and have a manager search for you on the internet or type your name into Google and find an image or something disturbing enough to stop the interview process. When candidates are interviewing, I always recommend keeping it private or deactivating it for the interview process so you can be extremely focused on winning the job, remember you're representing your last name and if you are fortunate enough to win the job, you'll be representing the employer in everything you do so keeping

your social media pages private is a part of showing professionalism.

5. **_BE EARLY, NOT ON TIME_**! – When I was an athlete we had a saying and I lived by this for 4 years, "If you're early you're on time, if you're on time then you're late, and if you're late, YOU'RE IN TROUBLE." The same rule applies to the face to face interview. If you're late to the first in-person interview and the manager is waiting there, chances are their mind is already made up, so it's extremely important that you show up at least 20-30 minutes early so the manager knows you're serious and you're ready to win your job. Not all managers are cut and dry but assume they are and show up early, remember it will separate you from the competition. Especially if you're in a bigger city and have to account for things like freeway traffic or taking another method of transportation like a subway or train.

6. **Look the Part** – You must be buttoned up, clean, and polished. More importantly look the part of someone successful. I always recommend male candidates wear a blue/black suit or for women candidates a black or blue pant-suit or dress, because blue and black are power colors and those colors show that you mean business and you're ready to win. If you look at any big-time sales meeting, the C-level executives and board members are always in a blue or black suit because they mean business. It's

important you mean business and look the part the minute you get out of your car and step into the organizations interview room.

7. **<u>Own The Room with Confidence</u>** – This is important for any candidate interviewing in any sales industry. When you're walking into someone else's arena for the first time, you want to display that you have the confidence and have what it takes to win the job. Before you sit down and meet the manager face to face for your interview, you're going to be walking in and sitting down and waiting somewhere. But when you're walking in, It all starts with your body language, facial expressions, and how you enter the interview room. People can sense when someone is either full of confidence and mentally prepared, or lacking confidence and unsure of their ability as a candidate. If you've ever seen the hit television comedy *Friends*, there's a great episode in season 7 when Susan Sarandon guest stars and coaches one of the main characters Joey Tribiani on how to "Own the room", and display the confidence needed to let the audience know that his character he's portraying should be taken seriously. She tells him "As soon as you walk into the room, you have to display the right body language, posture, and look". This can be applied to the interview process. If you walk in and display the right amount of confidence, look professional, you'll feel like $1M, people will feed off your

energy, and the people you're greeting first like the receptionist will know that you mean business and are ready to go for your interview. Remember, like Susan Sarandon says during the show, "When you walk into the room, don't be mad at the room, own the room."

8. **Use the Sales Process in Your Interview** – The sales process applies to the face-to-face interview in many ways. Build a rapport with the manager the same way you would build a rapport with one of your clients. Make the environment comfortable for yourself to sound confident when you interview. Use the research you've done on the company to talk about it with the manager. Use your current job to help talk about yourself and show the manager what they're getting if they bring you on their team. From your end, try to make the interview conversational and have a nice flow to it. You can do this if you're prepared thoroughly to win the job.

9. **Have a Professional Folder with Your Resume/Brag Book** – It's important to remember that first impressions are everything, especially during the face-to-face interview. I always recommend candidates to have a nice folder (Black or brown colored leather folders are the best) with a notepad for taking notes during the interview, 3 copies of your resume and your bag-book so you're prepared to go over everything from top to bottom. I think it's

important to bring 3 copies of your resume; in-case the manager throws a curve ball by having another manager in there. If you have 3 copies then each of you can have a copy of your resume to go over together.

10. **<u>Have Letters of Recommendation or Linked-In Recommendations</u>** – Having letters of recommendation to go with your resume is huge. I always recommend candidates to have at least 3-5 letters of recommendation showing how well you've done your job and what you bring to an organization. It's good to have different types of recommendations too. For example, if you can walk into an interview and have a recommendation from a co-worker, your manager you report to, and a respected client that you've done business with, then the manager is getting 3 different perspectives of recommendations which really shows 3 different perspectives of you as a candidate. Also, it's important to note Linked-In recommendations are just as strong as letters of recommendations since this is the digital age and social media plays a big role in companies hiring candidates now. There's no limit to how many recommendations you can have on your Linked-In profile so if you can get a healthy amount of them before you go on an interview, it always helps and will make you look stronger to the hiring manager.

11. **Have a Brag book** – It's important to bring a brag book to the interview to show proof of the accomplishments you've put on your resume or the awards you've won from your current employer. It helps you stand out from the competition and it helps you build a rapport with the manager. It's also great marketing for yourself as a candidate and it makes you feel more confident throughout the interview process. The information should be in a nice folder or in a hard binder so it looks professional when you give it to the manager to review.

12. **Have a 30-60-90 day plan** – Some managers might not require this on an interview but as a candidate, always assume they'll ask for one and have it ready to go in your professional folder. Wait for the manager to ask about what you'd want to accomplish in the first few months on the job and bring it out to show what your plan is. You may decide not to use it in your first interview but it's great to have in case you need to bring it out. Remember to be realistic in your 30-60-90 plan when you're preparing it, by preparing an action plan for your first 3-6 months on the job it shows the manager how serious you are about winning the position. Common 30-60-90 day goals are learning about the product/service, training, meeting your current customers and asking for referrals from them, finding existing sales

opportunities and new sales opportunities, following up on leads, meeting team members that are successful, building your pipeline, and closing the opportunities in your pipeline.

13. **Take Notes** – This shows that you're serious and you care about the position and company you're interviewing with, managers will take you seriously if you take the interview seriously and taking notes is a big part of that. Managers will be taking mental notes on you from the minute you enter in to the minute you leave, and it makes a great impression if you can walk out of that interview with a few pages of handwritten notes to use throughout the rest of the interview process.

14. **Ask a Good Amount of Questions** – Asking questions is important during the face-to-face interview with the manager. It shows that you're engaged and you've done your research on the company, products/services, culture and growth. When a manager asks you during the interview "what questions do you have?", always be sure to ask as many relevant questions as you can. Don't overwhelm the manager with questions but bring a good amount that shows how serous you are about the position. Sound confident while you're asking the questions you've prepared and make sure you take notes when the hiring manager gives you answers to those questions.

15. **<u>Use Your Current Sales Position to "Springboard Yourself"</u>** – This is extremely important during the interview process. Sales managers love hearing about how your hardcore B2B sales training or current sales position has helped you evolve and grow as a sales rep. Most smart candidates will use what they've learned from their past hardcore sales jobs and use it as a way to springboard themselves to the next step of the interview process with the employer they're interviewing with. For example, → "I learned how to prospect from my fortune 100 B2B company and having that type of sales training will help carry over into the next step of my career when it comes to prospecting for new business, using the sales process, building a rapport with clients, and more importantly generating revenue for our team." You're showing the sales manager how your sales training will carry over for your next step by providing a clear example of what you learned in your previous position and how you can apply it to the next step of your sales career.

16. **<u>Sound Confident when Talking About Yourself, not cocky</u>** – Do you remember seeing *Star Wars Episode IV: A New Hope?* In that movie there's a scene when Luke Skywalker and Han Solo are shooting imperial tie fighters from Han Solo's ship, the Millennium Falcon. Luke quickly destroys a few enemy fighter ships out of the sky, gets overly excited and keeps saying "I got him! I got him!" Solo sternly replies,

"Great Kid! Don't get Cocky!" His message is simple, if you're cocky while you're fighting then you'll lose the battle and we'll be gone. Interviews can be like that scene from Star Wars, they are exciting and fun, especially when it's your turn to talk about yourself. However, It's important you do not sound arrogant, especially to a manager that's the decision maker. The last thing a manager wants to do is listen to someone that sounds arrogant or overly confident in an interview. Sound confident in who you are, what you've done, and what you're bringing to the organization that's interviewing you. Do not blame your current organization for you looking for a new sales career. Managers will hesitate to hire someone if a candidate starts playing the blame game and blames territory growth, issues with the manager or company, or basic opinions of your job. Internalize when you're on the interview process and talk about why you've decided to start a new career search. ***Remember, selling yourself is the hardest thing to sell*** and the right amount of confidence (Not cockiness) you have in yourself, the more appealing you're going to come off to the hiring manager.

17. **Make the Interview Conversational** – Have you ever been on a first date with someone for a meal or coffee and the conversation with the other person just flows naturally? It's a great feeling, right? There's no nervous energy in the room, it calms your mind

down and you're not afraid to open up to the person that's across from you on the date. The date becomes conversational and both people on the date can let their guard down and feel comfortable. The same principle can be applied to the Interview process. As a professional sales candidate, if you can make the interview with the manager conversational and free-flowing, it will give you a better chance of winning the job you're interviewing for. You can do this by using what I call the *"Interview Garden Theory"* which means you have to dig deep to find a common ground with the manager, ask some good questions, and get the manager to open up to you. Also, when the interview becomes conversational, that's your chance to close the manager the first time (remember you might have to close more than once on an interview) and ask for the next steps of the interview process.

18. **Find Your Motivation to Share with the Manager** – Remember every candidate brings something unique to the table when they're interviewing for a job. If a manager asks you what motivates you to get the job tell them the factors that come into play for you, but don't sound basic. Don't say the basic things like money, success, and lifestyle, a manager hears that all the time and they want to hear something unique or outside the box. A unique example would be *"My motivation for getting into medical device*

sales has been there since day one of breaking into the sales industry. I love to help people daily and make a difference and this is the only industry that offers that every day. The devices you sell to hospitals and doctors impact patients lives everyday and that's something that has always been important to me throughout my sales career."

19. **Have that "IT FACTOR"** – I tell candidates that are prepping for interviews the "IT factor" stands for **Intelligence/Intellect, and Tenacity**. People wonder who has the "IT factor" and the truth is EVERYONE has the "IT factor"; the candidates that recognize this are the ones that pull it from the inside of them and use it during the interview process and win their sales jobs (think 80/20 rule). It's inside of every candidate and they have the potential to bring it out of them to impress a hiring manager during the interview process, but it's up to you as the candidate to recognize that you have what it takes to WIN the job; you have to apply it in the interview process.

20. **ALWAYS BE CLOSING!** – This is the most important part of your face-to-face interview. You've been in there for a while meeting with the manager and checked all the boxes and this is the most important box to check for this stage of the interview process. Remember, candidates that do not close the manager usually do not move forward during the interview process, it's something managers always look for even if you just had the greatest interview of your

life, the manager will still be looking for you to close him/her and ask for the next steps of the interview process. Even if the manager won't hire you on the spot, sound confident in your ability to close and ask to move forward to the next step of the interview process. When the manager thanks you for your time and asks if you have anymore questions; that's the best time to close them on the spot. Example close: **"I want you to know, I'm extremely interested in joining your sales team and working for your organization. Everything we went over today aligns with my career goals and strengths as a candidate and I see myself being a top-performing sales rep for your organization. What hesitancies do you have with me as a candidate moving forward in the interview process?"** It's important to note that managers might not show emotion or enthusiasm when you're closing them, don't let that throw you off, they're simply testing your will. Think about the "Batman Begins" movie we talked about in chapter one, when Ras'Al-Ghul is training Bruce Wayne to become batman, he constantly tells him "Your will is everything!" The same principle applies to the interview process, your will to close and be great is everything to move forward along with your preparation, and managers will feed off your will along with your attitude/energy/effort if you're serious about moving forward. Stick to your game-plan and keep closing them, show them that you're serious about moving forward in the interview process.

21. **Thank You Email** – Before you leave the interview, ask for the manager's business card. Send them a thank you email **on the same day** detailing your interview with the manager. The email should give a recap and end with a closing statement to the manager re-iterating that you're serious about the job. The Thank you email should look something like this- **"As I mentioned in our interview today, I believe my strengths, experience, and determination make me a great candidate to join and make an impact on your organization. Thank you for your time today and I look forward to the next steps of the interview process."** Once a manager sees a thank you email then they'll either tell a recruiter or tell the candidate directly if the candidate is moving forward in the process.

Action Items – The Face-To-Face Interview

1. Are you preparing yourself properly to meet, interview, engage with, and CLOSE the hiring manager and the employer that's going to be interviewing you for the next steps of the interview process? Remember as a candidate, preparation is everything and managers/employers sense when a candidate is prepared or unprepared for their interview.

2. Have you done your research on the company, products/services you'll be selling, the hiring manager you're meeting with, and do you feel confident enough in your ability as a sales candidate when you meet with the employer/manager to tailor your answers so you're giving yourself the best chance to WIN the interview you're on?
3. Are you prepared to close the hiring manager multiple times and show them why you're the best decision for the organization and the position you're interviewing for? Managers will be waiting for you as the candidate to close them for the next step of the interview process.

CHAPTER 6

THE FIELD RIDE/DAY IN THE LIFE OF A MEDICAL DEVICE SALES REP

> "It's not about the destination; it's
> about the journey to get there."
> – VICTORIA ORSINGHER

The Ride-Along/Field Ride – Usually after a face to face interview with the manager, you're going to do a field ride with one of the reps, it typically lasts all day or at least half a day. A field ride gives potential candidates a "day in the life" of what the job will be like. Even though a manager won't physically be there, they'll have eyes/ears everywhere and they'll tell the reps you're riding with to give them a full report of how the day went. It's important to treat the field ride as you would an interview with the manager because on the field ride, the rep you're shadowing becomes the decision maker. It's important to be just as energetic and engaged with the rep as you would with the manager. In this chapter I'll break down the tips for winning your ride-along/field ride with the rep you're shadowing and advancing to the next round of the interview process which is the final Interview. Here are some tips below to helping you WIN the field ride part of the interview process.

1. **Arrive early for your meeting with the rep** – *Treat the rep like you would treat the hiring manager.* The rep you're shadowing will be the decision maker for the day and you want to make sure you're ready to go from the minute you meet until the minute the field ride ends. This means being early, NOT on time, it's important to remember the rep that you're shadowing is going to be taking mental notes and will be reporting everything back to the manager that happens during the field ride. Arriving early will show the rep that you're serious when it comes to winning the job and it will set the tone for you to have a great field ride and ultimately close the rep/decision maker for the next steps.
2. **Build a rapport with the rep** – If you can build a report with the rep then it will make the field ride smoother and more engaging for you as the candidate. Ask the rep what the agenda will be during the field ride and what expectations should be. Some reps will explain it but some will also be waiting for you to engage them and ask them what the game-plan is for the field day. Let your personality come out after

you meet the rep and build a rapport with him/her. Share your story with the rep and explain why you're trying to join the organization and what your long-term goals are for your sales career. Listen to the rep when you're getting advice on how to do the job effectively and how the rep has progressed with the organization and what tips he/she has for you on how to be successful at the job so you can become part of that top 10-20% of the sales-force.

3. **Turn Your Cell Phone Off** – This is important, the phone needs to be off, not silent but completely shut off. Part of engaging with the sales rep you're shadowing in the field is having 110% attention to detail and it's important to remember there are going to be eyes/ears everywhere that day when you're in the field and texting/calling someone while you're on a field ride is a cardinal sin in the managers eyes. It's also good etiquette to turn your phone off during the field ride, a rep could take it as a sign of disrespect if they see you texting/calling the majority of the time during the field ride. Of course If you need to check on something for work or a personal/family situation, then simply ask the rep if you can excuse yourself to check for emergencies with work, etc.

4. **Challenge the rep in a professional manner** – Part of challenging the rep you're shadowing is doing things like asking sophisticated questions about the company, products, and the job duties itself. Step

outside your comfort zone and make sure you're doing your part during the field-ride. If you can get the rep to see that you're more than just a sales candidate and you have an agenda because this is the job that you want, then they'll be more inclined to open up to you and give you their endorsement to the manager as a solid candidate for their team.

5. **Volunteer to sell the products on the Field Ride** – If the rep you're shadowing let's you sell to one of the call points during the field ride, or even lets you ask questions to one of the call points, you should definitely do it. Do not be afraid to roll up your sleeves, get your hands dirty and sell, it's all part of the process, and remember if you honor the interview process it will give you a better chance to win the job. It also gives you an opportunity to show the rep your selling skills and it gives you practice so if you get the job, you'll have an idea of how the medical devices/services are sold and what techniques to use. Remember the managers will have eyes/ears everywhere and if you pass on the opportunity to try and sell during the field ride, the manager will almost certainly find out about it and it could put a negative image of you in their head.

6. **Don't get too comfortable** – Even though you'll be out of the office all day on a field ride, this is still an interview. It's important to not let your guard down and stick to the professional script of interviewing.

Mostly everything you talk about with the rep during the field ride should be related to the company, products, job, etc. Be careful if the interview becomes conversational too. Sometimes managers/reps will turn an interview into a conversational interview and they'll wait for you as a candidate to slip up and say something that might turn them off. It's important to keep the interview professional because it will make you look good as a candidate and it will give you a better chance of winning the job.

7. **CLOSE THE REP FOR NEXT STEPS** – Remember at this point in the interview process you've met with the hiring manager, shadowed a territory rep in the field, and experienced a "day in the life" of the job you're hoping to WIN. In order to advance to the next step of the interview process (usually the final interview); you need to close the sales rep the same way you'd close the hiring manager from your prior interview. Make sure to ask the rep for a business card if they have one so you can send the rep a thank you email. Also, it's important to note that you should get a recommendation from the rep so you can use that in your thank you email to the manager and the rep.

8. **Send a Thank You Email** – There's two different ways you can construct the thank you email for this part of the interview process. Some reps do one email and copy the rep and the manager on it,

others do 2 separate emails. There's no perfect way to do it, and ultimately you want to do what makes you feel comfortable, but the important thing is that the email goes out to both decision makers – the hiring manager and the rep you shadowed in the field. Apply the same principles you used in your closing email to the manager but make sure to email both parties involved. Remember to close the rep and the manager again in the email. Reiterate that this is the job for you and your day in the field with the rep validated that more. Here's an example closing email to the rep/manager – *"Hi Steve and Derek – Derek thank you for having me in the field today and for making time to fit me in your schedule. It was a great learning experience watching you sell the devices to the doctors and seeing you in action during our time together. Steve I want to thank you for having me shadow your top rep Derek in the field today. It was a pleasure meeting him, learning about his journey as a medical device sales rep, and visiting clients with him. After shadowing Derek in the field and seeing a day in the life of one of your sales reps, I realize this is the sales position I want and this is the organization I want to join. I want to thank you both again for having me and I look forward to the next steps of the interview process. I hope you both have a great rest of your week."*

Action Items – Field Ride

1. Are you prepared to see a "day in the life" and what the job entails that you're interviewing for?
2. Did you learn a lot from seeing how much activity the rep is doing everyday out in the field and what it takes to be successful as a medical device sales rep?
3. Have you done your research on the sales rep you're shadowing and have you prepared questions for that rep? Getting to know the rep's story/journey and building a rapport with the rep is vital to moving forward in the interview process. Candidates must get the reps approval to move forward to the next step of the interview process.

CHAPTER 7

THE FINAL INTERVIEW

> "Be the BEST version of you."
>
> – ANONYMOUS

The Final Interview – The final step of the interview process is usually meeting with a regional sales director or VP of sales, companies will determine who you need to meet with during a final interview. Everything you've done up to this point will need to be reviewed again and buttoned up a little bit more so you're ready to win your job and more importantly, win your sales career.

The big thing to keep in mind during this part of the interview process is to not get content and remember to always keep your foot on the gas. Michael Jordan, the greatest basketball player of all time has an awesome quote about winning. *"I play to win, whether it's during practice or a real game. And I will not let anything get in the way of me and my competitive enthusiasm to WIN."* As sales candidates, you can apply this same way of thinking to the final interview. You are in there for a reason and the job is yours to win, and at this point nothing can get in your way of winning the job except for yourself.

But it's important to note that before you have your final interview, find new ways to brush up on company information, questions you've asked the manager and ways to close, so ultimately you can walk out of there with a verbal job offer from the decision maker. Here are some tips below for WINNING the final interview.

1. **Build a Rapport with the VP** – It's important to build a rapport with the highest executive you'll be interviewing with. You want to make sure you do this first before jumping right into your questions you have for him/her. Assume the VP or regional sales director doesn't know anything about you and will be judging you based off their first impression of you as a professional candidate. It's important to maintain the same hunger/attitude that's gotten you to this point of the interview process with the highest person on the sales team. Chances are they'll be asking you how the interview process has been going and usually that's when you can share what the managers, reps and other people involved have told you up to this point of the interview process.

2. **Wear a Power Suit** – I think it's important to bring this tip back to the final interview because you want the VP of sales to know that your primary objective

is to walk out of that interview room with the verbal offer and wearing a power suit will only help your cause. As I stated earlier most decision makers or board member wear hard-hitting power suits in a board meeting. If you take that mentality and apply it to the interview with the VP of sales, then it will give you more confidence going in and a better chance to win the job.

3. **Stick to Your Game-plan** – You've come to the finish line of the interview process, don't make things complicated. Stick to what you got you here to this point – the preparation, the experience required to be considered for the job, and you showing them why you're the best fit for the position. Continue to review your prep work and make sure it's buttoned up and fine-tuned to meet with VP of sales then go win the job.

4. **Tailor Your Interviewing Questions** – Don't ask the same questions you did to your potential manager or the rep you shadowed in the field ride. Remember you're going to be dealing with a VP of sales or Regional Sales Director so make them more sophisticated and structured for a higher level audience. Center them around topics like long-term growth or long-term direction of the company or the division you're interviewing with. A regional sales director or VP of sales will be waiting for you to ask them well thought-out questions and what type of effort you put into your preparation to meet with them.

5. **<u>Be Prepared for a Mock Sales Presentation</u>** – As you get deeper into the interview process for a medical device sales job, managers and employers will challenge you to think outside the box and show them why you're the best choice possible for the job. Usually most medical device employers will put their potential candidates through some type of a Mock sales presentation to see what your selling skills are like and to see how prepared you are, the setting could go a few different ways. I've seen it be something simple like selling the managers your phone or selling them the bottle of water they hand you. Or the setting could be equivalent to a hospital and they'll be acting like doctors and you'll be responsible for pitching/educating/selling/closing the product. It's important that you do your research on the products and know what the functionalities are of the products/devices you'll be pitching during the final interview. Sometimes I've seen managers have a panel that includes multiple managers and a rep that might be your future co-worker that you'll be selling the devices to. Make the presentation interactive and engaging to the panel of interviewers. Treat it like you would treat a sales call that you've gone on for your current position. Make sure the content is great when you present and your timing is great too, managers will respect a candidate that has a polished presentation. Remember the more

prepared you are for this part of the final interview, the better of a chance you'll give yourself to ultimately WIN the medical sales job.

6. **CLOSE THE VP & ASK FOR THE JOB** – This is the last real test you'll have in the interview process. After you've gone over everything with the VP of sales, the last thing to do is close him/her and ask for the job. Everything you've done up to this point will be tested when you meet with and eventually close the VP of sales. It's important to note that as a candidate, you should close the VP of sales the same way you would close the hiring manager and the rep you met with for the field ride, with the same professionalism and closing ability you've shown throughout the steps of the interview process. Be sure to bring up everything you've accomplished throughout your sales career up to this point and make sure they know how serious you are about joining their organization and what you can bring to their team. After you've closed the VP of sales, send a follow up thank you email thanking them for their time, close them again in the thank-you email and ask for the job.

Action Items – The Final Interview/Interview Process Recap

1. How Prepared are you for sales interviews? Compare your preparation with a friends preparation and see how you can help each other going forward.

2. Are you doing the little things to honor the interview process, win your sales job and ultimately win the sales career you want?
3. Do you feel that you are "wow-ing" the decision makers or managers you're interviewing with during the interview process? If not, how can you improve?
4. Are you ready to face key decision makers during the interview process and show them what you bring to an organization and make sure they know they're getting the best candidate possible for the job?

CHAPTER 8

THE RIGHT PROFILE AND PATH TO TAKE TO BREAKING INTO MEDICAL DEVICE SALES

> *"By choosing our path we choose our destination."*
>
> – MONSON

The Medical device sales industry is a well-known career destination that hundreds of thousands of candidates are trying to break into everyday. But, to get into the medical device sales industry, there's a certain path/profile that hiring managers and most successful med sales reps have taken not just to break into the industry, but find sustainable success and build a successful sales career.

Any medical device sales recruiter will recommend you take the traditional medical sales path to give yourself the best chance of breaking into the industry (college degree, entry level sales job, hardcore outside b2b sales job, no job-hopping on the resume, and a hardcore sales personality).

There's also a certain profile that hiring managers are looking for in potential candidates for medical sales.

When I say specific profile, I want everyone reading this to think of the online dating industry for a minute. If you've ever used popular dating websites like match.com or eHarmony.com, you have tools you can use to filter out the type of dating partner you're seeking on those websites. If they don't meet **YOUR** criteria, then you filter out the bad eggs and find someone that does meet your criteria. Why is this important? It gives you a better chance at meeting someone, starting a relationship, getting married, being happy, etc. The same thing is true in the medical device sales industry, there's a specific profile these managers are looking for from candidates that are interviewing for their respected sales positions, and if you don't fit the manager's profile/criteria, then most likely you won't get your chance at interviewing for a medical device sales job.

In this chapter I'll break down the proper steps to take to get into the medical device industry and list the companies that can help you break into the industry so you have a clear direction on how to break into the medical device sales industry.

These are the steps that are required to take the traditional path to break into the medical sales industry:

1. Graduate from a university with a 4 year bachelors degree
2. Work at an entry level sales job to build your resume

3. Work at a hardcore outside B2b sales Job to build your resume, get professional sales training, and learn how to sell and close.
4. Don't be a Job-Hopper
5. Have a Professional Linked-IN Page.
6. Have a type A/hunter Personality
7. Break into medical sales as an associate sales rep or full line rep

1. **Graduate from college with a 4 year bachelors Degree** – This is extremely important for any candidate interviewing in any sales industry, let alone medical device. Med device companies are cracking down and tightening up their requirements for candidates to have a chance at breaking into the industry and having your college degree is an important requirement. I've heard managers say that even if a candidate has hardcore sales experience but has no degree, they're reluctant to hire the candidate or most likely won't hire the candidate at all. Med device managers want reps that are well educated with 4 year college degrees. The 4 year degree is important because it shows that you have the ability to start something and complete something important at a young age.
2. **Find an Entry level sales job** – As you explore the world you'll see there are a lot of opportunities for employment, especially in sales. The medical device

sales industry looks for candidates that have a good amount of experience and it starts with taking the right kind of entry level sales job. Now sometimes there are rare occasions where recent college graduates will get an entry level medical sales job, but it's important to remember that 9/10 times that won't be the case. Usually if that happens it's because they either did an internship with that company as a student, or participated in a program where the medical device company was specifically looking for a recent college graduate and the expectations might be different for the graduate than they would be for an associate sales rep or full line territory rep. Some great entry level sales jobs out of college are ***Enterprise-Rent-A-Car, Avis-Budget*** (also a rental car company), and ***Gallo Wine Company***. They typically hire college graduates and have entry level training programs that help build sales skills and your sales resume.

3. **Find a Fortune 500 HARDCORE OUTSIDE B2B Sales Job** – When you're reading this step, please know this step is **VITAL** to breaking into the medical device sales industry. I capitalized the word **VITAL** because as a candidate, you need to know how important this step is to breaking into the medical sales industry or any hardcore sales industry for that matter. There are so many boxes these jobs check for candidates just by being an employee at

one of them. Hardcore b2b sales jobs **give you paid fortune 500 sales training, teach you the sales process and how to use it, build your resume, give you a chance to sell products/services and interact face-to-face with the decision makers, and more importantly hardcore B2B sales jobs help open doors up to the next step of your sales careers like the medical device industry.** To have a fortune 500 B2B sales company on your resume when you're interviewing for a medical device job will give you the candidate a much better chance at winning a medical sales job and breaking into the industry on your terms. Think about this aspect of it too – as consumers of retail products, we typically buy well-known brands that we trust right? Brands like *Mercedes Benz, Apple, Samsung, Ralph-Lauren, Nike, Under Armour, Adidas, etc.*, have a history of getting the job done and making us feel like we made the right decision when we purchased one of their products. Hiring managers take the same approach when they're hiring candidates for these hardcore med device jobs. They hire from B2B companies they trust because of the factors I listed above here. It's important to note that when you're going through this process to *make sure the hardcore B2B sales job you decide to take is in outside sales, not inside sales.* Phone sales is an art too, but medical device companies typically don't hire inside sales reps because there's no face-to-face interaction

A MILLENNIAL'S GUIDE TO BREAKING INTO...

at an inside sales company. Here are some fortune 500 outside b2b jobs that can help give you a better chance of breaking into hardcore medical device sales. Keep in mind these are in no particular order so as a candidate you can join any of these and they will give yourself a good chance of breaking into the medical sales industry. Keep in mind too it will help you break into the medical sales industry if you go to one of these companies and perform well and exceed expectations while you're there (presidents club, sales awards, promotions) because you can add these accomplishments (See chapter 3 for this section too) to your resume going forward:

ADP – Fortune 500 payroll/HR solutions
Paychex – Fortune 500 payroll/HR solutions
Cintas – Fortune 500 Uniform/facilities services
Unifirst – Fortune 500 Uniform/facilities services
Aramark – Fortune 500 Uniform/facilities services
Ricoh – Fortune 500 Copier/Printer sales
Xerox – Fortune 500 Copier/Printer sales
MRC Technologies – Copier/Printer Sales
Konica Minolta – Fortune 500 Copier/Printer sales
Toshiba Business Solutions – Fortune 500 Copier/Printer/Office hardware sales
Staples B2B – Office supplies/equipment (This is not the retail company, this is a different division)
AT&T Telecom – B2B telecom/hardware/software

Verizon Telecom – B2B telecom/hardware/software

Sprint Telecom – B2B telecom/hardware/software

4. **Don't be a Job-Hopper!** – The average sales candidate stays at their job for 6-10 months then leaves to find a new job because they're usually not happy, not making money, or just want a new situation. That's not even enough time to give the job a real chance. Hiring managers from Medical device companies want candidates that have a history of progressing throughout their career and showing they can move up the corporate ladder, but they don't want people that are leaving after every 6 months to find something new. Hiring managers want candidates that will stick out a job for minimum 2-3 years and grow within a company, get promoted, win some sales awards, hit some type of conference or presidents club and show that they're capable of growth and achieving success. Remember, when a medical device company brings you on as a sales rep, they're investing 6 figures in you to train you with the expectation that the ROI (Return on Investment) will be much bigger long-term and with hopes that you'll be a top-performing sales rep.

5. **Have a Professional Linked-IN Page/Profile** – This rule applies to all social media, but especially linked-in. Usually one of the first things a hiring manager does after we send them a candidates resume is

search for them on social media/linked-in and see what their profile looks like, if it mirrors the candidates resume, and if the candidate has a professional linked-in page. I always encourage candidates to take this seriously because managers want people to join their team that are extremely professional. It's important to make your social media pages private while going through the interview process. In the new era of interviewing and digital media, Linked-In is becoming the new resume and Linked-In recommendations are becoming the new forms of written recommendations that managers are looking at so it's important that you the professional sales candidate take this seriously and have a professional linked-in page from top to bottom. This means having a professional profile picture, the right contact info, a nice well-written summary about yourself/what you've done throughout your professional career and what you're looking for, having some linked-in recommendations (if you have written recommendations those are ok too) from people that appreciate your work like successful client stories, customers, co-workers that value you on their team and if you can have one from your manager.

6. **Type-A Hardcore Sales Personality** – This quality goes back to chapter 4 when I talked about how to win the interview, but I wanted to bring it up again because it's important to winning a job, and it's

related to the profile that these hiring managers from med device companies look for when they're hiring sales candidates for their team. The B2B sales training that you'll get from the companies listed above will help you deal with call points going forward like various types of doctors, hospitals, surgery centers, treatment centers, etc. Typically, most reps that break into medical sales learn how to build relationships with the decision makers but those hardcore hunting skills you learn from the B2B training will come into use for the rest of your sales career. Managers want to hire candidates that are gung-ho, driven, motivated, have shown previous success, and have that "IT" factor that they can bring with them to an organization. If you're not Type-A that doesn't mean you're going to eliminate yourself from getting a medical job either, but it does help having that type of hardcore sales personality or mentality when you're interviewing, and those B2B sales companies help your personality adjust for the next step of your sales career.

7. **Breaking Into the Med Device Company** – It's important to note to find a med company that fits your personality. There are so many different types of medical device employers out there but a good amount of them make you sacrifice for a few years on the job. For example, if you take a job at a Fortune 500 medical device company like Stryker in

one of their trauma divisions, you might be required to work on-call hours at 1-4AM or on weekends for the first 6-18 months of the job. If you're a candidate that's serious about medical sales you have to do your homework and find out what company fits your personality. Do you want to sell capital equipment or disposables? Do you want to work on-call for the first year or do you want to work at a smaller company and work an 8-5 schedule Monday-Friday? Would you ever consider selling a medical service? Would you consider working for a start-up medical company? These are questions to ask yourself when you're going through the interview process because as sales reps we're constantly building our resume and aiming towards the future with future opportunities. Now, once you break into the medical device sales industry, there's a few options you have as a rep. Typically what you'll find is most reps from the hardcore b2b sales companies break in as ASR's (Associate Sales Reps) unless they're performing at such a high level and making a solid 6 figures and wind up taking a job as a full line rep, but in order to do that you have to really be a top performing outside B2B sales rep. Also, it's important to remember if you start off as a full line medical device sales rep or full line territory rep with a higher base salary and higher compensation package, there's more pressure on you to sell/deliver results right away, the money is higher but with more money, comes more responsibilities. If you start off as an associate sales rep you can learn the game and observe everything first hand, work under a senior territory manager (make sure to use them as mentors too so they can help get you prepared for what's next), understand the wording to talk to doctors and not feel overwhelmed when you break into the medical device industry, then progress naturally throughout your medical sales career.

8. **Finding the Medical Device Job Before "THE Job"** – This factor can certainly come into play throughout your medical device sales career, especially when you're just starting your medical device sales career. In the medical device sales industry, the top 10-20 companies to sell for usually have a line of candidates wrapped around the building waiting to get their shot to work for them. When I was a sales candidate I was fortunate enough to interview at a few top 20 medical companies simultaneously. One of the sales managers I interviewed with told me I had "tremendous potential to be a high 6 figure rep in the industry", but he was worried that I wasn't ready to handle the workload, pressure, and responsibility of a full line territory rep position. So he recommended that I look into an associate sales position so I could "get my feet wet" for a few years and understand the responsibilities of a medical device rep

and then be ready for that job in my future. If you're a candidate interviewing for a top 20-40 medical company and you don't get a job there after the first try during the interview process, don't get discouraged. The best recommendation I got and that I can share with you is to find a medical company that can help you break into the industry and find success so when that right medical sales job comes knocking on your door, you'll be ready to handle all the responsibilities that come along with the job.

Action Items – The Right Path and Profile of a Medical Device Sales Rep

1. What type of sales are you in now?
2. Do you have B2B sales training? If not, look into those companies, that will give you a better chance of breaking into medical sales
3. Are you a job hopper? If you are, challenge yourself to stay at your job for at least 18 months – 2 years so you can build your resume and look solid on paper
4. Do you have a hardcore sales personality? Remember managers are going to be looking for candidates with that "hunter mentality" as they look to build their team. It's important to have that trait in your personality because there is hunting in medical device sales.

CHAPTER 9

THE MILLENNIAL EFFECT IN SALES

*"We don't have to be great to start,
but we have to start to be great."*
— ZIG ZIGLER

I love the quote above to start this chapter by Zig Zigler. In case you don't know who he is he's the motivational speaker, world renowned author, and of course, one of the best Salesman to ever walk the earth. His quote means we all have to start somewhere and find the courage to take that leap and have enough faith in ourselves to find success in our careers. The hardcore sales world is a lot like the quote from Mr. Zigler. We all start somewhere, and if we work hard enough, (especially as millennials) then we'll find an industry that will give us a chance to take off and fly, and ultimately become successful sales reps, or whatever career path you decide to pursue.

It's important to note as Millennials, we have to be careful and selective with our career choices. In 2016, the

Harvard Business Review noted traits and trends that could help our generation going forward. The journal noted that "6/10 millennials leave their jobs at the beginning of every year to explore other opportunities, and the opportunities are not within the current company". "71% of Millennials are not engaged or actively disengaged at work, making our generation the least engaged generation in the U.S." There's another side to this story too. The Harvard Business Review notes our generations "willingness to switch jobs and companies presents a substantial attraction opportunity for organizations."

It's also important to note about what our generation of Millennials look for in potential jobs and job searches. The Harvard Business Review article from 2016 notes that our generation puts an emphasis on factors such as *opportunity to learn and grow, the quality of manager, the quality of management, and most importantly the interest in the type of work that we're doing* (HBR, 2016).

The great thing about the hardcore medical device sales world and sales world in general is that there's a storm coming in the next few years, and it's all of us, the millennial sales reps. Our generation of millennials (And yes for those of you wondering, I am a millennial too) now make up the biggest slice of the American workforce, and it's only going to get bigger for years to come, pretty crazy right?

In fact, recent articles from well known publications like Forbes have said by 2020, 50% of the American workforce will be millennials, and by 2025, 70% of the workforce will be made up of millennials. It's been said by Lee Caraher, the San Francisco based author that *"A business without millennials is a business without a future."* Think about that for a second, a company survives based on sales and production of sales by their sales reps. A company's future depends on our generation of millennials and how much we can drive sales in our respected organizations. That's a big deal (in a good way of course) going forward for all of us and it's a clear indication that every millennial candidate out there reading this will have an opportunity to take off and fly in the wonderful world of hardcore sales.

As millennials, we possess the qualities that organizations look for when they're interviewing candidates for hardcore sales jobs. We're hungry, tenacious, hard-working, goal-oriented, and driven to be successful, it's ultimately up to you as the candidate to prove that to an employer and show them why they should invest 6 figures in you and make you a part of their organization. We have found ways to get ahead of the curve with apps, technology, and applying these to our everyday lives. If you the candidate take the same approach to the interview process, you will continue to give yourself a better chance to win a sales career and find success in the medical sales, or any hardcore sales industry you choose to pursue.

CHAPTER 10

MY CLOSING WORDS

> *"Closing thoughts are so you know,
> Final. Let's call them closing words."*
> – CRAIG ARMSTRONG

Before I share my closing words with you, I want to say thank you to everyone that read my book *"A Millennial's Guide to Breaking Into Medical Device Sales"*, and to everyone that has given me a chance to help them break into the medical device sales world. The support from everyone means a lot and I have a genuine passion for helping people across the country which is why I became a medical device sales recruiter.

I'm sure after reading everything about the medical device sales industry, the steps to get into the medical sales industry and sales world in general, you might be feeling a little overwhelmed and asking yourself "Is this the right career path for me?" or "Am I making the right decision by entering the world of hardcore sales?"

The answer is an overwhelming YES. I want to direct you back to 2 quotes that all potential sales candidates should think about everyday when they're interviewing for the hardcore sales job they want. The first quote is from Earl Nightengale and I mentioned it in Chapter 1 of this book: "Selling is the world's highest paid profession, IF we're good at it, and if we know where we're going." The second is from chapter 7, The Final interview: "Be the BEST version of You".

Both these quotes provide meaning and substance on multiple levels because if you have a passion for selling and making a difference and if you train yourself to become great at it, you will give yourself a better chance of breaking into any sales industry let alone the medical device sales industry.

So now what? You've read everything from why you should break into sales, to what a career in medical sales can do for you, to the profile these companies are looking for. It's important to note that some people reading this "How-To" guide might decide a career in hardcore sales, especially in medical device sales might not be for them, and that's okay, like I said earlier in this book, as a candidate, you should always do what makes you feel comfortable and what you feel is the best option possible for your career. More importantly, you should always find a job that will make you the happiest because that will ultimately lead to you finding some type of success.

But my hope for all of you that read this is that you've learned the right path to take and the secrets to not only interviewing for a medical device sales job, but WINNING the medical device sales job and ultimately WINNING your medical device sales career.

Everyone reading this "How to Guide" is part of the next great wave of great sales reps, whether you choose to break into hardcore medical sales or another industry is entirely your decision. But it's important to know the impact that all of you can have on the sales industry in general, it's bigger than you think. Companies survive based on sales, and they need great reps to survive and grow over time. As Millennials, knowing we're such an important piece to this is extremely motivating to help as many people as we can find success in the hardcore sales world.

Yes there is a path to break in and a profile that these managers are looking for, and while it is an up-hill climb to break into the medical device sales industry or any part of hardcore sales for that matter, if there's any generation that can make the climb and find success, it's our generation because we're well educated, driven to be successful, and have a plan that we can follow.

When it comes to the medical device sales industry, honoring the interview process and following the plan of attack is vital to not only winning the medical sales job, but ultimately finding success in the medical device sales industry and winning your sales career. As a Medical device sales recruiter, our job is to find the right talent and connect them with the right opportunities in the medical device sales industry, and my goal is to ultimately help as many of you as I can out there, point you on the right direction and give you the right tools to give yourself a better chance of breaking into the medical device sales industry. In closing I'll leave you with the words of Earl Nightengale's *Strangest Secret In The World*– "Become the person you want to become. Start today, you have nothing to lose, but you have a whole career to *WIN*."

-David Bagga
The *MILLENNIAL* Sales Recruiter
#WinYourSalesCareer

www.ingramcontent.com/pod-product-compliance
Lightning Source LLC
Chambersburg PA
CBHW070051210526
45170CB00012B/659